Aromatic Perceptions

Aromatic Perceptions

—————————— Vincent Blaison ——————————

RESOURCE *Publications* · Eugene, Oregon

AROMATIC PERCEPTIONS

Resource Publications
An Imprint of Wipf and Stock Publishers
199 W. 8th Ave., Suite 3
Eugene, OR 97401

www.wipfandstock.com

PAPERBACK ISBN: 978-1-6667-6286-0
HARDCOVER ISBN: 978-1-6667-6287-7
EBOOK ISBN: 978-1-6667-6288-4

11/28/22

Contents

Preface

This is my second poetry collection following my first book, *Awaken*. After opening my eyes to truth, this book focuses on the wisdom God continues to teach me. I hope that my words and experiences may bring light to others and glory to God. Life is a river, constantly flowing, it will forever continue to shape me.

I want to thank each and everyone of you that takes the time to read these words and support my work. I am very grateful for those who surround me and help to continue to refine me. Without you, I am nothing. I want to give a special thanks to my old team-Armando Canales, Saje Flores, Mary Richards, Antonio Sandoval, Kelsi Johnson, David Her, Matt Gheno, Bee Hernandez, James Lewis, Jose Salazar, Martin Rosales, Jon Elias, Rafael Haulk, Jack Parkansky, R'Rheana Vazquez, Dewey James, Gavon Yang, Matheson Thor, Eugenio Avila, Monica Duran, Samantha Clevenger, JJ Antonio, Doug Castro, Daniel Alvarado, Jaeden Brown, Brodey Pinto, and Brandon Agtang. Also, a huge thanks to my wife Ashley, my son Elias, and my great friend Bryce Cruz. I have grown so much with the time I've spent with you all, and I hope I may have done the same for you.

Traveler

The gears clicking and clacking
The hands move forth
Traveling through time
Floating through the breeze
Some moments
Missed in the mist
Of the midst of being lost
Buildings fallen
Cities rebuilt
Finding our paths
With faith through the dark
The sound of flapping wings
Breaks the silence of the course
I seek to reach the Heavens
Of God Almighty's Throne

Life

The ups and downs
Silhouettes of perceived standards
Perception dismayed
Unto photographies of past, present, and future
Who shall we become?
I begin to walk on my own two feet
Infallible decisiveness
Spinning in circles
Yet somehow continuing forward
Battles of dark and light
Sheathing each breath
To uncover raw wisdom
Within the dust of diamonds
The story is only beginning . . .

Growth

Ancient languages
Spoken, yet unheard
Absorbed
Into guidance
Through the trials

Eyes renewed
To view the old world
Reborn
Yet, only seen
From my own
Conscious views

Realities
True or false
Are only my own
Creations
With constant
Evolution

Molding the pot
Carefully
With every motion
Permeating
With deep meditation

Delving deeper
Into the rabbit hole
Expanding consciousness
To arrive
At expected locations
And walk into
My awaiting fate

Still A Bit Groggy

Inceptions of a dreamlike state
Awoken from the slumber
Overcome the fear created coma
And rise with renewed belief of true possibility
The system glitches with each
Meticulously placed step
Vision cleared to see the symbolic pattern
Of "reality", now plugged into the source
Synaptic thunderstorms swirling in motion
Follow the path that is laid before me
Seemingly unable to grasp just yet
Destiny begins to form in existence
Once blurred vision now comes into focus
Pieces of me picked up along the journey
Tomorrow will soon become today

Welcome

Soulfully grounded
As my mind attempts
To drift into tomorrow

Finding contentment
In every situation
Through gratitude

Blessings in each moment
Viewed through absorption
Of release of control

Just as a heart beating

With every beat
Melodies of echoing love
Fill the absent
Pieces of my soul

This house is now a home
And for you
Now, an open door

Hmm . . .

Contemplation of consciousness
Subsidized levels of clarification
Molecular structures of self-made reality
Visions of what could be, push to become
To dream in the awakened state
Uncovering truth to what has always
Lied before us
This *is* the dream before we "fall" back asleep
Into unconscious subconscious
Where trees fall off the leaves
Leaves me to wonder . . .

In Session

Placed in atmospheric storms
To push past limits of self
Battles within myself
To attain oneness
Facing the heart of ego
Which lie within my mind
Truth at constant evolution
Consistently breaking barriers
Previously unbreakable
Each step with renewed strength
As the mind utters wondering fears
Journey through the valleys and pastures
I will make it to fate's court
Finding strength in the midst of struggle
I will soon complete this new course

Blank Canvas

The blank canvas awaits
For the story to be written
For the brush to be stroked
For the picture to be framed
For the memory to be engraved

Steps must be taken
While thoughts must be given
To birth action, from a beautiful dream

Stillness in the mind
To hear symphonies of silence
And be encompassed
In the wisdom of the waterfalls of knowledge

Each glimpse of art
Lived through each moment
Shall splash upon life's canvas
And leave its mark as another sign
Of God's Glory

Just Be

Delving deeper into the depths
At times, so focused on the intricacies
Mind, set on achieving

I miss the beauty of simplicity
I miss the beauty of what is
I miss the beauty of now

I once viewed the true greatness
Of the architectural grand scheme
With each stroke of art before me
At a constant complete loss for words
But routine enters and many a time
Taken for granted
Familiarity dulls the senses
So I must deaden the inanimate
Attention seeking idols
So beauty, may once again be revealed

Hike

Traversing the meandering path
Unaware of what lies behind each turn
Each decision filled with blind faith
Scales constantly tipping
Blindfolded, as I read under the Sycamore Tree
Gusts of wind breeze through like sunshine
Breaking through the leaves on a hot summer day
Refreshing, yet, sometimes, unnerving
Placing my path where my path has been placed
Forgiveness found at birth's origin
Each word, each line, so meticulously placed
Progressively unlocking more provoking thoughts
With each turn of the page
Placing the bookmark at the end of this shift
So I may sit and catch my breath

The Fall and Rise

Knowledge of silence
Brings wisdom of still waters
The testing of the test
Breaks through
As levels of comprehension
Rise with heavy rainfall
Storms of purposeful destruction
Transformed to form
Growth now grasped
Judgements left behind
As views pierce through false truths
Attaining knowledge of nothingness
I rise further into the clouds

Address Change

Perceived vision blurs truth of atmospheric sights
Logs removed, now reveal green pastures
Where once desolate wastelands roamed rampant
The truth of "I" fails to interpret comprehension
Where is, what was, and what shall come to be
All contained in confrontation and release of all
To approach the fear of fear—acceptance
It's truth transcends all that is presently known
To create new worlds with unscathed lands
This shall be my new home

Refinery

Expectations of conceptual thoughts
Seeking to find what we believe to find true
Blind to see what continually lies before our eyes
Attempts to grasp what is already held within
Separation further increases
Deceived by blurred reflections
Progressing to attain that which leads us astray
Unknowing, lacking senses of known wisdom
We must release self to find guidance
Casting out all that which lacks in faith
Overbearing pressure while heat rises
The refinement process continues
Soon, a diamond shall emerge
And the ashes, blown away

Writer's Block

Thoughts conflicted
Doubt creeps in
Blocking the flow of wisdom
Yet, only the thought of doubt
Creates the doubt
Placing false barriers
Self holding self
Limits bow and break
With rising belief
Yet, the shattering
Is only containment
Of once believed belief
Breaking the pot
Of once restricted roots
We are now free
To become

Focus

Waking up from dreams of past realities
With the scent of shameful mistakes
A reminder, it's not too long ago
And always one decision away
So I keep my eyes locked up
And my heart full of faith
As to not stray away
If you slip upon your path
It is your own doing
A hand stretched out
Is a spirit lifted up
Voices dissipate
Through constant surrender
Trusting Jesus while blindly walking
The mustard seed grows

Oxygen

Illusions of the grasped
Never truly holding one thing
Just a creation of thought
Manifested into "reality"
Bubbles drifting up
In the depth of inceptions of the sea
Flipped upside down
As we drown
Above water

Renewed Eyes

Belief is key
Unlocking travesty
To leave past tragedies
To heal while finding burdens
To become blessings
In seasons
Of once thought droughts
Stories of confliction
Cliffhangers built of tear drops
While teardrops of wisdom
Pour into the cup
Overfilling with love
As we see now
With true vision up above
Gates open
As we ascend to new heights
We're welcomed home
Thank God for this new life

Wisdom Whispers

Frozen in motion while moments arrive within centered awareness
Logs pierce through the blinds as sleeping minds
Awaken through broken mirrors
Splashing truth once forgotten, from disbeliefs birthed from pains
Love returns us home as street lights flicker, beckoning
    for our return
This journey through the subconscious neighborhoods
Traversing our own self-inflicted wounds
Battles in the valley, healing roots of the Great Sycamore
Breaking through new ground in this new land approaching
She is confident in our future as cities are rebuilt on
    concrete foundations
"Zion, Zion, Zion", she whispers, as the clouds bring about
Renewing rains for the drought
Trust and you will find, believe and you will see the true way
We're just about home, love will always find a way

Chess

Further down the path
As the aroma of fresh coffee beans
Permeate the air
My grogginess
Slowly begins to fade

I rise up out of bed
A peculiar game of chess
Anxiously awaits my first move
The board filled with conflict
Each move seems to pierce my finger
With painful, transcending intent

Each piece strategically placed
Yet, my opponent, unseen with each move
Discipline provides consistency
As I progress forward
In this silent battle

The closer I become to victory
More pawns are sacrificed to create distraction
Whirlwind of monopolies
Shedding fear of the unknown
My knight rides forth

Check.

Visual Eyes

Expectations of what we believe to be true
The view of what we seek is much further than the truth
Misguided eyes to unsee with farsighted vision
Focus comes into focus when vision is lost from past whence
Manifestations of said born realities
Riddles in the mist yet unraveled and placed before us
Deconstructed to be picked up along the path
Circles in forward motion, while taking steps back to progress
Time's moment of clarity, when comprehension surpasses
    understanding
The surrounding atmosphere creates gravitational fates
While each moment quakes with newfound growth
The blade breaks through concrete
The water erodes the impenetrable
The light breaks through darkness
Paths open, with a new way

Expansion

Rivers expanding as synapses spark growth of roots
Consciousness of consciousness, inceptions of truth
Lightning branches outward as knowledge is gained within
Emptying myself to be filled with true depths of living water
Puzzle pieces to be pieced together with universal connectivity
Wisdom rises with the downfall of self, pushing away to arrive
Contradictive correlations reveal constitutional laws of the ancients
Push past the walls of the wind to view the sea with spectacles
    of clarity
The density, but a spec of sand, blown away with perception of time
The weight, far too heavy to carry, yet leaning against the foundation
Becoming light as a feather
Rise, the warriors of light stand once again
The revolution has just begun
With new beginnings, come new ends

Piquancy

Awakening to truth, a new world before me
New challenges with never ending distractions
Though I ponder . . .
Maybe these distractions are direction
For supplementation of the coming
To find contentment in every situation
Seems tediously unattainable
Each single moment, seemingly separated from the next . . .
Yet, somehow intertwined within the mind
As I meander forth through this metaphorical forest
Each step filled with piquant wisdom
Pulling me in with its alluring aroma
Where shall this scent of sense lead me?
Faith filled steps into unknown depths
Somehow I can now breathe underwater
Distractions yet again arise
New perceptions lead to old views demise
Evolving into new creations
The limitations of no limitations
The belief of a growing mustard seed
Still . . . oh so still
Still, as the ripple sent forth from a splashing rock
It shall meet its destination only true to its truth
Wisdom placed so eloquently in plain sight
Welcome to the new world
For those with proper eyes

Eye of the Storm

Seeking guidance of the silence
Amid bellowing distractions
The next step, covered in growing brush
Meditative states, while chaotic tunes ring
The eye of the storm only discovered
Whilst enduring the relentless rains
Which direction to choose?
For each moment presented
Faced with different faces of sacrifice
Uncomfortability must transcend
To limits of comfort
Difficulties rise with new levels attained
While grasped with flowing sand
Through crevices of aging fingers
Pointing to destinations reached
From evolution of the mind
Thoughts drop like dimes
The rain begins to pour
Passing upon the moments
Where beauty hides within her shell
Longing for the moment
The self-portrait comes into focus

When The World Came To Life

When the world came to life
Color transformed
The once known black and white
When the painting showed truth
Of the artist' strokes of life

Oh, when the world came to life
And my darkness turned to light
When love showed through
Breaking through the past pains
That held back living life

Yeah, when the world came to life
Jesus reached down from Heaven
To save this lost life
Though, a much painful journey
Of faith through action
To arrive next to His side
I can never thank Him enough
For this truly blessed life

Beauty is Pain

Beauty is pain
Pierced from a thorn
Withered like a petal
Destined for more

A heart full of pain
Tattered and worn
Staggering through the streets
From now, till evermore

Yet, a new day shall begin
With rebirth in sight
The dawn sheds the darkness
The once dead, rise again in life

Hopelessness dissipates
As strengthened wings reach to the Heavens
Pain processed for progression
True beauty formed through the fire

Flower

Move forth towards progression
Lean into uncomfortability
To break once known barriers
Set new standards
As growth can no longer be contained
Planted into new soil
Heavy rainfall coaxes the seedling
It shall burst forth through foundations
And begin its ascent
Towards destiny of being
It can only be
What it is
It can only
Be

Free Spirit

Eloquence presented her
Striding through the fields in a white dress
Arms spread wide
As her fingertips caress the petals of a rose
Dancing amongst the angels
Her love permeates through the silent moments
Free, free as a bird
Spinning in elegance as her hair flutters in the wind
Life gravitates towards her luminescent light
Her love
Oh her love
Gives me strength
To continue the fight

Sands of Time

Each moment passes like a gust of wind
Each granule of sand drops with immeasurable weight
The depth surpasses comprehension
The rushing sand blares tunes as that of a raging waterfall
Echoing bittersweet symphonies of chaos and beauty
Perception of time kneaded like dough
Stretched and spilled with gravitational pull of revolving doors
Atmospheric containment shatters
For possibility could not be contained within the hourglass
Inceptions of a desert
Becoming what already is
As each spec of sand drips
Touched by another to alter its evolution
Growing in expansion until oneness is attained
Moving as one, it flows with current and wonder
Destined to be reunited
Under the sun

Fork in the Road

One life, filled with a multitude of lifetimes
Everything we know is true
Is only fictitious theories
Based upon obscured facts
A thousand years passed by
As I awaited to rise with the living
I sat with death, unknowing I enjoyed its company
Then, finally, truth shimmered in my eyes
And my vision blurred, almost lost
The veil started to rise
Uncovering a world I only viewed in dreams
Presented with a choice
To choose life or death
Still, somehow, difficult to make a decision
I had no strength, but hope flickered in abundance
I began to rise out of my grave
A vessel of light, His strength filled me
I shed myself for your sake
My charity will spread through the land
I am here, now

Message Clock

Constant contemplations of which thoughts should spill
    onto the platter
Battles of patient eagerness storm my mind with
    unrelenting contradictions
"Now is the time" (but is it?)
.... (should I wait?) ....
Jump
.... (so tired ..... so much to do ..... not now ....) ....
Time ....
What is time? ....
Ticking
Ticking
Ticking
Echoing wonder through the roots
Does fear hold me back?
Fear of success?
Fear of the unknown depths?
Yet, the waiting seems to sprout weeds in the garden
But faith is my gardener
........"Be still" ....
The sound ripples through my weakness
Stilling the rough waters of my doubt filled mind
Do not stare at the sea
For you will not see the beauty of the ocean
Be one with the moment
Become the breeze
Brisking across the waves
As the wind envelopes you in motion

With You

Open my eyes to see the true beauty which lie past the twinkle
    of a star
Open my eyes to the true grandness of each passing moment
Let me delve into the symphonies of silence
And dance in the clouds as sunshine trickles upon my spirit
Let me get lost in your eyes as I peek into the universe in still motion
Let me kiss your lips as our souls illuminate the moment
As we embrace each other and existence pauses
A glimpse into Heaven is caught
When I am with you

Mindspace

Thundering thoughts with flowing visions
Pouring wisdom upon the planes of DNA
In evolutionary motion
Inflating an empty world within battles of self
Becoming a new creation
While transcending the sky's ocean
Possibilities destroying limitations
Placed by limits of known knowledge
Exasperating the bubble of worldly wisdom
Circular motions transforming the clay pot
Filled, but empty, without presence of knowing
Walk through the valley while deepening roots of selflessness
Evaporating into the universe
Weaving self into all

Guided Path

Pebbles placed along the path
Picking them, piece by piece
Each leading to new knowledge
Uncovering new lands awaiting to be discovered
Every thing, somehow universally connected
Wisdom reveals herself within a patient bloom
Flowering the surrounding soil
With seeds of life eager to sprout
New eyes within the mind of openness
Viewing the familiar with constant evolution
Growing fascination with eager hopes of finding truth
I continue forth in this journey
Paths always leading to you

New Day

Wisdom wakes as eyes dawn upon a new day
Constant battles within the mind's war as self overcomes self
Transcending dispositions as blurred copies of true self
Slowly come into focus
Each day rises with renewed strength
Found within yesterday's pain
Gratitudes of difficulties pleases maturity of spirit
Growth quakes through ages, breaking ground as Zion rises within
Metaphorical metaphors shower acidic rain on once believed beliefs
Shackled by limitations of majority's mask
Dissolving false views from pessimistic tunes
Rise, rise, rise, like those before you
Step into the clouds as destiny approaches
Sail into the unknown depths of the sky's ocean
Find your place among the stars
And illuminate through the darkness

Aroma

As I awaken to the aroma
Of an empty cup of coffee
My senses indulge
In this newfound piquant world

A simple sip of the cup
To become filled with emptiness
I dissolve within its permeating aroma

The transformation of mind
Brings new eyes
Which leave behind
The guise of a past character
Now departed

My presence shall become
One with the rising sun
And my voice shall echo
Through the silence

Your Timing

Difficulties
Of waiting on your timing
Trying to be present in the moment
As my mind travels into tomorrow
So I must be still as the trees
And allow the wind
To pull me in

Stumbling Blocks

Trying to find a balance
Battles of complacency and yesterday's standards
With visions of standing atop conquered mountains
The old self pleads with tempting shouts of return
The future self ponders with anticipating hope

To uncover pure joy within my daily defeats
Societal definitions of insanity
Plague awaiting cleansing waters
Though the rapids would surely destroy my vessel
True faith is found in walking on water

On my path I will stumble, and surely, I will fall
Though dust shall not settle on my journey
As the storm clouds brew above my spirit
I continue forth and bid fear farewell

Concrete Ceilings

Distorted vision
Of troubled days
Pushed to extreme pressure
Not to break
But for concrete ceilings
To burst
So the sproutling should grow
Through concrete ceilings
Of self-made limitations
Held down by false belief systems
Created in adolescent
Birth of traumas
Evolving into
Maturing ego
The veil now removed
Uncovering truth
Now the light
Shall bring a new day
Keep watering the roots
To destroy
Concrete ceilings

Snare

You catch my eye with a twinkle
Pages turn to find you are always there
The truth behind my blind eyes
Your love captures me like a snare

Failure

Pain pushes complacency
Gathering inner strength
To overcome previous lost battles
Failure still present
To reach out its hand
So we may rise
With renewed strength
Somehow, victory is found
In the midst of failure
Earthly vision
Proves true to distortion of truth
Seeking to find
Pure joy in difficulties
While insanity sounds preceding
Wisdom beyond ages
Pierces through limiting beliefs
Of an adolescent mustard seed
For what we perceive
Manifests into
What shall become
To feed the mind
While blindness consumes the eye
Should lead us astray
Yet, patience pursuing that which is received
Should prove truth concluded
Through selflessness

In the Midst

What is truly seen in the midst of just a moment?

A shower in the sky
Yet somehow
Our eye misses
The beauty of each droplet

What is truly seen in the midst of just a moment?

For if we could just pause time
Would we then be able to see the beauty held
While viewing life from this battle-scarred shell?

What is truly seen in the midst of just a moment?

For what we seek seems to slip past us
As we long for the once present moment
It was here, before our eyes
Yet, destination corrupted our focus

What is truly seen in the midst of just a moment?

Be still and close your eyes
And release your minds forward pulling motion
Let your view rest upon the sky
For love permeates within each wave of the ocean

Lens of Love

Blind me so that I may see
To perceive reality as it truly is to be
To push past myself
So I may see the true you
To truly love in the way
That shows my heart to be true
For if I can truly love me
Surely, I can love you

Metamorphosis

Stages of metamorphosis
Becoming in the midst of becoming
In the eye of the storm
Whilst being molded
From past and future self
Molded with each moment
From the potter's hands

The clay spins in wonder
As the shape takes form
Each line, each movement
Filled with detailed purpose
For us to uncover at fate's rendezvous

Prismatic foundations
With vibrational balance
Shifting with each moment
As ego fails to conquer
While the memories placed ahead
Light paths to a once known
And soon to be yet again
Destination

Could You See as I?

Through the eyes of each single life,
What truly lies before us?
I wonder, could you see as I?
For I surely could not see as you . . .
What lay upon the vastness of your eyes
As each owns reality seeps out
With each intimate moment
Untainted from a world's eye view
As true spirit surpasses physicality's atmospheric bondage
Finding the key to unlock genuine expressiveness
Without shadows of self, creating separation of identity
What truly drives our hearts?
Do we seek peace inwardly or outwardly?
Yet, many a time ignorant to shackled freedom
Walking blindly to our fall
For what we seek, truly, we shall find
Wisdom peaks through crevices
As light shines upon our adolescence
Truth is found through blank pages
As written words distract the mind
To seek death is to find life
For our vision is truly deceiving
For who I am begins to rise through layers of ash
Once buried for survival
I wonder, could you see as I?

www.ingramcontent.com/pod-product-compliance
Lightning Source LLC
Chambersburg PA
CBHW071741020426
42331CB00008B/2118